Get slim
cookbook

igloobooks

Published in 2014
by Igloo Books Ltd
Cottage Farm
Sywell
NN6 0BJ
www.igloobooks.com

Food photography and recipe development: PhotoCuisine UK
Front and back cover images © PhotoCuisine UK

FIR003 0514
2 4 6 8 10 9 7 5 3 1
ISBN 978-1-78343-467-1

Printed and manufactured in China

Get slim
cookbook

Contents

Introduction

Prepare to cook yourself slim with the Get Fit for Life Cookbook, an essential food bible for those who want to look and feel their very best all year round. Explore new flavours and delicious food combinations, with over 50 recipes to keep you satisfied and nourished throughout the day.

For fanatic foodies who love nothing more than filling their homes with wonderful aromas, then you will not be disappointed with these exquisite, healthy recipes. Including Breakfast, Lunch and Desserts as well as Snacks and Drinks, these recipes are ideal for a post-workout energy boost.

Breakfast

Breakfast is a highly important meal and should ideally be packed with fruit and fibre to support your system and provide slow-release energy throughout the day. There are so many tasty choices that can complement any lifestyle or fitness regimen.

Choose the Strawberry, Pear and Mint Smoothie for a light, low-fat option or try the Salmon and Egg Galettes, perfect for a hearty weekend brunch shared with friends and family.

Top Tip

Try serving the salad with a side of fat-free Greek yoghurt.

Fresh Fruit and Coconut Salad

Serves: **4** | Preparation time: **40 minutes**

Calorie content: **138 cal/portion**

Ingredients

- 1 small pineapple, trimmed with skin and core removed
- 300 g / 10 ½ oz / 2 cups strawberries, hulled and halved
- 1 tbsp stevia or granulated sweetener
- ½ lime, juiced
- a few drops of vanilla extract
- 30 g / 1 oz / ½ cup coconut flakes

Method

1. Cut the pineapple into slices and then into cubes.

2. Mix with the halved strawberries, stevia, lime juice and vanilla extract in a large mixing bowl.

3. Cover and chill for at least 30 minutes.

4. When ready to serve, spoon into serving bowls and top with coconut flakes.

Melon and Ham Cold Salad

Serves: **4** | Preparation time: **15 minutes**
Calorie content: **111 cal/portion**

Ingredients

- 2 small Cantaloupe melons, halved horizontally
- 150 g / 5 oz / 1 cup air dried lean ham slices
- ½ red pepper, deseeded and very finely sliced
- ½ small cucumber, deseeded and very finely sliced
- ½ small red onion, very finely sliced
- 1 small bunch of basil, leaves picked
- salt and freshly ground black pepper

Method

1. Scoop out the seeds from the insides of the melon halves and discard.

2. Using a sharp paring knife, cut out teeth patterns around the perimeter of the melons.

3. Use a melon baller to scoop out balls of melon flesh and reserve to one side.

4. Line the melon halves with some of the ham before arranging the melon balls, finely sliced vegetables and more ham on top.

5. Season with some salt and black pepper before garnishing with basil leaves.

6. Serve cold.

Top Tip

Try crumbling over a little reduced-fat feta cheese for a salty tang.

Top Tip

Instead of using sun-dried tomato, try chopped, drained artichoke hearts.

Egg, Tomato and Bacon Sauté

Serves: **4** | Preparation time: **15 minutes**
Cooking time: **10–15 minutes** | Calorie content: **145 cal/portion**

Ingredients

- 55 g / 2 oz / ⅓ cup sun-dried tomatoes
- 1 tbsp white wine vinegar
- 4 small eggs
- 4 rashers of turkey bacon
- non-fat cooking spray
- 300 g / 14 oz / 6 cups spinach, washed and dried
- 4 spring onions (scallions), finely chopped
- salt and pepper
- a few sprigs of chervil

Method

1. Place the sun-dried tomatoes in a bowl and cover with hot water. Leave for 10 minutes to reconstitute then drain, patting dry, and chopping.

2. Preheat the grill to hot and place a grilling tray underneath.

3. Bring a large saucepan of water to a simmer before stirring in the vinegar. Poach the eggs at a simmer for 3 minutes then remove and drain on kitchen paper.

4. Grill the bacon on the hot tray for 2 minutes on both sides, or until golden and crisp. Remove and drain on kitchen paper.

5. Coat a large sauté pan with cooking spray and place over a moderate heat until hot.

6. Add the spinach, onions and 2 teaspoons of water. Sauté until the spinach is wilted then drain on kitchen paper and arrange in serving bowls.

7. Top with sun-dried tomato, a poached egg, a rasher of bacon and a sprig of chervil before serving.

Scrambled Eggs with Toast

Serves: **4** | Preparation time: **10 minutes**
Cooking time: **2–3 minutes** | Calorie content: **227 cal/portion**

Ingredients

- 8 small slices of white bread
- 4 large eggs
- 55 ml / 2 fl. oz / ¼ cup semi-skimmed (2%) milk
- ½ tsp mixed peppercorns, crushed
- salt
- non-fat cooking spray
- a few chive stalks, snipped

Method

1. Toast the slices of bread in batches until golden-brown on both sides. Remove to one side as you prepare the eggs.

2. Beat together the eggs with the milk, crushed peppercorns and some salt until thoroughly beaten.

3. Spray a non-stick frying pan with a few sprays of cooking spray and sit over a medium heat until hot.

4. Once hot, add the beaten eggs to the pan and cook, stirring frequently, until softly scrambled, about 2–3 minutes.

5. Stack slices of toast on serving plates and spoon the scrambled eggs into small pots, then garnish with chives and serve with the toast.

Top Tip

For an added touch of luxury, try serving the scrambled eggs with some fat-free crème fraiche on top.

Top Tip

Try a sprinkling of chopped pecans or walnuts instead of sunflower seeds for a nutty crunch.

Oat and Yoghurt Muesli

Serves: **4** | Preparation time: **5–10 minutes + chilling time**
Calorie content: **217 cal/portion**

Ingredients

- 110 g / 4 oz / 1 ¼ cups rolled oats
- 125 ml / 4 ½ fl. oz / ½ cup cold water
- 125 ml / 4 ½ fl. oz / ½ cup skimmed (0%) milk
- 1 tbsp sultanas
- 1 small Red Delicious apple, roughly grated
- 55 g / 2 oz / ¼ cup fat-free plain yoghurt
- 75 g / 3 oz / ½ cup raspberries
- 55 g / 2 oz / ⅓ cup blueberries
- 1 tbsp sunflower seeds

Method

1. Combine the oats, water, milk and sultanas in a bowl and stir well. Cover and chill overnight.

2. The next morning, stir in the grated apple and spoon the muesli into serving bowls.

3. Top with a dollop of yoghurt, a few raspberries and blueberries as well as a sprinkling of sunflower seeds.

4. Serve immediately for best results.

Whipped Quark with Honey

Serves: **4** | Preparation time: **5 minutes**
Cooking time: **5 minutes** | Calorie content: **146 cal/portion**

Ingredients

- 400 g / 14 oz / 2 cups quark
- 1 tbsp stevia or granulated sweetener
- 55 g / 2 oz / ¼ cup runny honey
- 100 g / 3 ½ oz / ⅔ cup raspberries

Method

1. Soften the quark in a mixing bowl before whipping with the stevia until creamy.

2. Divide between four serving glasses and top with honey and a few raspberries.

3. Serve immediately for best results.

Top Tip

The whipped quark can be covered and chilled for up to 2 days before serving with the garnish.

Top Tip

For an even healthier version, you can swap the bacon for rashers of low sodium turkey bacon.

Egg and Bacon Toasts

Serves: **4** | Preparation time: **10 minutes**
Cooking time: **10 minutes** | Calorie content: **187 cal/portion**

Ingredients

- 4 small slices of white bread
- 4 rashers of back bacon
- non-fat cooking spray
- 4 small eggs
- 50 g / 2 oz / 1 cup baby spinach, washed and dried
- salt and freshly ground black pepper

Method

1. Preheat the grill to hot and place a grilling tray underneath.

2. Toast the bread. Use a large flower-shaped cookie cutter (or any other shape) to stamp out shapes from the slices, set to one side.

3. Grill the bacon for 2 minutes on both sides until golden and crispy remove and drain on kitchen paper.

4. Coat a large frying pan with non-fat cooking spray and heat over a moderate heat until hot.

5. Fry the eggs in batches until the white is set but the yolk is still runny.

6. Place the toasts shapes on plates, top with a little spinach, then a folded piece of bacon and more spinach on top.

7. Top with the fried eggs and a little seasoning. Break the yolk if desired before serving.

Salmon and Egg Galettes

Serves: **4** | Preparation time: **40 minutes**
Cooking time: **15–20 minutes** | Calorie content: **231 cal/portion**

Ingredients

- 300 ml / 10 ½ fl. oz / 1 ¼ cups skimmed (0%) milk
- 6 small eggs
- 2 tbsp chopped fresh dill
- 100 g / 3 ½ oz / ⅔ cup buckwheat flour
- non-fat cooking spray
- 110 g / 4 oz / ⅔ cup smoked salmon slices
- ½ lemon, juiced
- salt and pepper

Method

1. Whisk together 225 ml / 8 fl oz / ¾ cup of the milk with 2 eggs, the dill and a little seasoning in a mixing bowl.

2. Add the flour and gradually whisk into a smooth batter. Cover and chill for 30 minutes.

3. Coat a small non-stick frying pan with cooking spray and heat over a moderate heat until hot.

4. Add generous tablespoons of the batter, spreading them into rounds with a spoon, before cooking for 1–2 minutes until bubbles appear. Flip and cook the other sides for 1 minute or until golden.

5. Keep the galettes warm to one side.

6. Whisk the remaining milk with the remaining eggs and a little seasoning in a bowl. Heat a saucepan over a medium heat until hot and cook the eggs, stirring, until scrambled.

7. Dress the salmon with lemon juice and serve on top of the galettes and scrambled eggs.

Top Tip

Instead of scrambled eggs, try spreading the galettes with fat-free crème fraiche and topping with salmon.

Top Tip

Try swapping half of the milk for plain fat-free yoghurt for a thicker consistency.

Strawberry, Pear and Mint Smoothie

Serves: **4** | Preparation time: **5–10 minutes**
Calorie content: **138 cal/portion**

Ingredients

- 445 g / 1 lb / 2 cups frozen strawberries, slightly thawed
- 500 ml / 18 fl. oz / 2 cups skimmed (0%) milk
- 1 small banana, chopped
- 2 small ripe pears, peeled, cored and diced
- a few drops of peppermint extract

Method

1. Chop one tablespoon of the strawberries and set to one side as a garnish.

2. Combine the remainder with the milk, chopped banana, pear and a few drops of peppermint extract in a blender or smoothie maker.

3. Blitz until smooth then pour into 4 glasses.

4. Garnish with chopped strawberry on top before serving.

Salmon, Poached Egg and Toast

Serves: **4** | Preparation time: **10 minutes**
Cooking time: **10 minutes** | Calorie content: **234 cal/portion**

Ingredients

- 1 tbsp white wine vinegar
- 4 small eggs
- 8 small slices of wholemeal toast
- 100 g / 3 ½ oz / ⅔ cup smoked salmon slices
- ½ lemon, juiced
- a few chive stalks
- salt and freshly ground black pepper

Method

1. Bring a large saucepan of water to a simmer and stir in the white wine vinegar.

2. Poach the eggs at a simmer for 3 minutes then carefully remove and draining on kitchen paper. Trim any strands of egg white and discard.

3. Toast the slices of bread until golden-brown on both sides.

4. Dress the salmon with lemon juice and a little pepper.

5. Sit the toast on plates and place the salmon and egg on top.

6. Season with more salt and pepper, garnish with chive stalks and serve.

Top Tip

Use gluten and wheat-free bread for a coeliac-friendly version.

Top Tip

A fine grating of orange zest on top lends an aromatic, citrus twist.

Summer Fruit Porridge

Serves: **4** | Preparation time: **10–15 minutes**
Cooking time: **10 minutes** | Calorie content: **217 cal/portion**

Ingredients

- 150 g / 5 oz / 1 cup raspberries
- 110 g / 4 oz / ⅔ cup strawberries, hulled and chopped
- 1 tbsp stevia or granulated sweetener
- ½ lemon, juiced
- 150 g / 5 oz / 1 ½ cups rolled oats
- 150 ml / 5 fl. oz / ⅔ cup cold water
- 150 ml / 5 fl. oz / ⅔ cup skimmed (0%) milk

Method

1. Combine the raspberries, strawberries, stevia and lemon juice in a mixing bowl. Stir well and cover, then set to one side for 10 minutes.

2. Combine the oats, water and milk in a saucepan set over a medium heat.

3. Cook, stirring frequently, until the oats start to absorb the liquid and swell. The porridge should be thick and creamy in consistency.

4. Spoon into serving bowls and stir through the fruit and any accumulated juices.

5. Serve immediately for best results.

Lunch

These wholesome lunches are simple and easy to make without fuss, but are incredibly tasty. Fill your plate with plenty of colour for a healthy, balanced meal. There are a number of delicious dishes which cater for a range of diets such as the Vegetarian Mushroom Burger, which will keep you full until teatime.

For something a little fancier, the Shrimp, Artichoke and Pea Salad is packed with flavour and only 120 calories per portion!

Shrimp, Artichoke and Pea Salad

Serves: **4** | Preparation time: **5–10 minutes**

Cooking time: **10 minutes** | Calorie content: **120 cal/portion**

Ingredients

- 300 g / 10 ½ oz / 2 cups whole shrimp
- 1 tbsp sunflower oil
- 400 g / 14 oz / 2 cups canned artichoke hearts, drained
- 125 g / 4 ½ oz / 1 ¼ cups mange tout
- 1 lemon, juiced
- 2 tbsp flat-leaf parsley, finely chopped
- salt and pepper

Method

1. Peel the body of the shrimp, leaving their heads and tails intact, before deveining them.

2. Heat the oil in a large sauté pan set over a moderate heat until hot. Add the shrimp with a little seasoning and let them sauté for 2–3 minutes until they start to turn pink.

3. Add the artichoke hearts and mange tout and allow them to warm through for 2 minutes over a reduced heat.

4. Add the lemon juice and reduce it a little then stir in the parsley and a little seasoning to taste.

5. Spoon into bowls and serve immediately.

Top Tip

A small handful of drained, preserved red peppers would be ideal added to the shrimp.

Top Tip

The bagels can be lightly toasted before assembling for a little added crunch.

Salmon and Cream Cheese Bagel

Serves: 4 | Preparation time: **10 minutes**
Calorie content: **302 cal/portion**

Ingredients

- 225 g / 8 oz / 1 cup fat-free cream cheese, softened
- a few chive stalks, finely chopped
- 100 g / 3 ½ oz / ⅔ cup smoked salmon slices
- ½ lemon, juiced
- 4 small seeded bagels, split in half
- a small handful of salad cress
- a few sprigs of dill, chopped
- salt and pepper

Method

1. Beat together the cream cheese, chives and seasoning in a small mixing bowl until thoroughly combined.

2. Toss the smoked salmon slices with lemon juice and a little pepper.

3. Spread the cream cheese onto the bottom half of the bagels and top with folded slices of smoked salmon.

4. Top with cress and dill then sit the top halves of the bagels in place.

5. Serve immediately.

Green Bean and Ham Salad

Serves: **4** | Preparation time: **15 minutes**
Cooking time: **16–18 minutes** | Calorie content: **120 cal/portion**

Ingredients

- 2 large eggs
- 200 g / 7 oz / 2 cups green beans, trimmed
- 100 g / 3 ½ oz / ⅔ cup cherry tomatoes, quartered
- 100 g / 3 ½ oz / ⅔ cup prosciutto slices
- 2 small shallots, finely sliced
- salt and pepper

Method

1. Cook the eggs in a saucepan of rapidly simmering water for 10 minutes.

2. Remove carefully and refresh immediately in iced water.

3. Place the green beans in a steaming basket. Cover with a lid and cook over a saucepan of simmering water for 6–8 minutes until tender.

4. Drain the eggs from the water before cracking and peeling carefully.

5. Cut into quarters and set to one side.

6. Remove the beans from the steamer and season then toss with the cherry tomatoes, prosciutto and shallot.

7. Arrange the salad in bowls before topping with quarters of egg and serving.

Top Tip

Try replacing the egg with flaked, cooked tuna and some pitted black olives.

Top Tip

Blue cheese such as
Stilton or Roquefort
would work equally
well in place
of Parmesan.

Corn, Tomato and Parmesan Slices

Serves: **4** | Preparation time: **5–10 minutes**
Cooking time: **3 minutes** | Calorie content: **186 cal/portion**

Ingredients

- 4 slices of white sourdough bread, 1 ½–2 cm thick
- 30 g / 1 oz / 1 cup basil leaves
- 100 g / 3 ½ oz / ½ cup canned sweetcorn, drained
- 4 large vine tomatoes, cored, deseeded and chopped
- 55 g / 2 oz / ½ cup Parmesan, finely shaved
- salt and pepper

Method

1. Preheat the grill to hot and place a grilling tray underneath.

2. Toast the slices of bread for 1 minute on each side before removing.

3. Finely chop a quarter of the basil leaves and set to one side.

4. Roughly mash the sweetcorn in a mixing bowl and stir through the tomatoes and chopped basil. Adjust the seasoning to taste.

5. Spoon the mixture onto the toasted bread and top with Parmesan shavings.

6. Flash under the grill for 1 minute before removing and serving.

Chicken and Fig Salad

Serves: **4** | Preparation time: **10 minutes**
Cooking time: **35 minutes** | Calorie content: **135 cal/portion**

Ingredients

- 2 medium chicken breasts, trimmed
- 1 tbsp sunflower oil
- 2 shallots, finely chopped
- 150 g / 5 oz / 1 ½ cups mange tout
- 50 ml / 2 fl. oz / ¼ cup red wine vinegar
- 4 ripe Bursa figs, quartered
- a small handful of basil leaves, roughly chopped
- salt and pepper

Method

1. Preheat the oven to 180°C (160°C fan) / 350F / gas 4 and line a baking tray with greaseproof paper.

2. Sit the chicken breasts on the paper and season the skin side generously before roasting for 20–25 minutes until golden-brown and cooked through.

3. Remove from the oven and leave to rest in a warm place, covered loosely with aluminium foil.

4. Heat the oil in a large sauté pan set over a medium heat until hot, then add the shallots.

5. Sauté for 2–3 minutes, stirring occasionally, before adding the mange tout and continuing to cook for a couple of minutes.

6. Deglaze the pan with the red wine vinegar, letting it reduce by half, then stir in the figs. Adjust the seasoning to taste.

7. Slice the chicken breasts and toss in the pan before spooning into bowls and garnishing with chopped basil.

Top Tip

Any soft stone fruit can be used in this recipe. Try apricots or peaches.

Top Tip

Top the patties with a dollop of light mayonnaise instead of chutney for a creamy addition.

Vegetarian Mushroom Burger

Serves: **4** | Preparation time: **20 minutes**
Cooking time: **40–45 minutes** | Calorie content: **294 cal/portion**

Ingredients

- 500 g / 1 lb 2 oz / 2 ½ cups canned chickpeas (garbanzos), drained
- 150 g / 5 oz / 2 cups chestnut mushrooms, finely chopped
- 1 tsp dried mint
- ½ tsp ground cumin
- ½ tsp ground coriander (cilantro)
- ½ lemon, juiced
- 2 tbsp sunflower oil
- 4 small sesame seed burger buns, split
- 2 tbsp tomato ketchup
- 55 g / 2 oz / 1 cup baby spinach, washed and dried
- 2 tbsp mango chutney
- 30 g / 1 oz / ½ cup beansprouts
- salt and pepper

Method

1. Preheat the oven to 180°C (160°C fan) / 350F / gas 4 and line a baking tray with greaseproof paper.

2. Cook the chickpeas in a saucepan of simmering water for 15–20 minutes until tender. Drain and mash well with the mushrooms, mint, ground spices, lemon juice and seasoning.

3. Divide the mixture into 4 and shape into patties then arrange on the baking tray.

4. Drizzle the patties with sunflower oil then bake for 20–25 minutes until golden on top.

5. Remove from the oven and leave to cool for a few minutes before assembling the burgers.

6. Spread the base of the burger buns with ketchup and top with spinach leaves.

7. Sit the patties on top and spread with mango chutney and top with beansprouts.

8. Sit the tops of the buns in place before serving.

Sautéed Vegetable Salad

Serves: **4** | Preparation time: **5 minutes**
Cooking time: **15 minutes** | Calorie content: **93 cal/portion**

Ingredients

- 2 tbsp sunflower oil
- 1 large white onion, chopped
- 1 large carrot, peeled and sliced
- 1 clove of garlic, chopped
- 2 small courgettes (zucchinis), sliced
- 110 g / 4 oz / 1 ½ cups white mushrooms, sliced
- 150 g / 5 oz / 1 cup cherry tomatoes, halved
- 1 tsp dried oregano
- 1 tbsp basil pesto
- 100 g / 3 ½ oz / 2 cups baby spinach, washed and dried
- 1 gem lettuce, chopped
- salt and pepper

Method

1. Heat the oil in a large sauté pan set over a moderate heat until hot.

2. Sauté the onion and carrot for 3–4 minutes, stirring frequently, until lightly coloured.

3. Add the garlic and continue to cook for 15–20 seconds before adding the courgettes and mushrooms.

4. Stir-fry for 3 minutes until lightly coloured then add the cherry tomatoes, oregano and basil pesto.

5. Stir well and cook over a reduce heat, covered with a lid, for a further 2–3 minutes.

6. Adjust the seasoning to taste and set to one side.

7. Arrange the spinach and gem lettuce in serving bowls and top with the sautéed vegetables before serving.

Top Tip

You can substitute the basil pesto for Thai red curry paste for an oriental twist.

Top Tip

This salad would work equally well with a cold, sliced chicken breast instead of salt cod.

Salt Cod and Orange Salad

Serves: **4** | Preparation time: **10–15 minutes**
Calorie content: **87 cal/portion**

Ingredients

- 200 g / 7 oz / 1 ⅓ cups salt cod, soaked in cold water overnight
- 1 large orange, peeled with white pith removed
- 200 g / 7 oz / 4 cups watercress, washed and dried
- 100 g / 3 ½ oz / ⅔ cup cherry tomatoes, halved
- 1 red chilli (chili) pepper, deseeded and thinly sliced

Method

1. Drain the salt cod and give it a quick rinse under cold running water before patting dry.
2. Flake the cod into a bowl and set to one side.
3. Using a sharp knife, segment the orange and collect any juice in a bowl along with the segments.
4. Toss the watercress, cherry tomato halves and chilli slices with the orange segments and juice, then divide between serving bowls.
5. Add the flaked salt cod before serving.

Baby Carrot and Coriander Soup

Serves: **4** | Preparation time: **15 minutes**
Cooking time: **30 minutes** | Calorie content: **71 cal/portion**

Ingredients

- 1 tbsp sunflower oil
- 1 onion, finely chopped
- 1 clove of garlic, finely chopped
- 1 tbsp ground coriander (cilantro)
- 450 g / 1 lb / 4 cups baby carrots, peeled and chopped
- 750 ml / 1 pint 6 fl. oz / 3 cups low sodium vegetable stock
- a few chive stalks, snipped
- salt and freshly ground black pepper

Method

1. Heat the oil in a large saucepan or casserole dish set over a medium heat until hot.

2. Add the onion and a little salt and sweat for 4–5 minutes until translucent.

3. Add the garlic and cook for 30 seconds, stirring, before adding the ground coriander.

4. Stir well and add the carrots. Cover with a lid and reduce the heat, letting the carrots soften a little for 5 minutes.

5. Cover with the stock once softened and bring to a simmer then let the soup cook for 15–20 minutes until the carrots are very soft.

6. Puree the soup with a hand blender until velvety and adjust the seasoning to taste.

7. Pour into mugs and serve with a few snipped chives on top.

Top Tip

A swirl of fat-free crème fraiche in the soup lends a pleasantly creamy tang.

Top Tip

For a vegetarian version, use cubes of pan-fried Halloumi instead of chicken.

Couscous and Chicken Salad

Serves: **4** | Preparation time: **15–20 minutes**
Cooking time: **10–15 minutes** | Calorie content: **232 cal/portion**

Ingredients

- 150 g / 5 oz / ¾ cup couscous
- 500 ml / 18 fl. oz / 2 cups low sodium chicken stock, hot
- non-fat cooking spray
- 2 medium skinless chicken breasts, trimmed and cut into strips
- 1 medium carrot, peeled and cut into strips
- 1 small courgette (zucchini), deseeded and finely diced
- 1 shallot, finely chopped
- 1 red pepper, deseeded and finely diced
- 1 medium vine tomato, diced
- 1 tbsp mint leaves, finely chopped
- 1 tbsp flat-leaf parsley, finely chopped
- ½ lemon, juiced
- salt and pepper

Method

1. Place the couscous in a heatproof bowl and stir in the chicken stock. Cover with cling film and leave the couscous to absorb the liquid for 10–15 minutes until tender.

2. Meanwhile, coat a sauté or large frying pan with 3–4 sprays of cooking spray and sit it over a moderate heat.

3. Season the chicken and sauté for 4–5 minutes until lightly coloured then add the carrot and courgette.

4. Continue to cook the chicken and vegetables over a reduced heat for 4–5 minutes until the chicken is cooked through and the vegetables are softened.

5. Fluff the couscous with a fork then stir through the chicken, carrot, courgette and remaining vegetables.

6. Add the herbs, lemon juice and adjust the seasoning to taste before serving warm.

Quinoa Tabbouleh

Serves: **4** | Preparation time: **10–15 minutes**
Cooking time: **15 minutes** | Calorie content: **211 cal/portion**

Ingredients

- 175 g / 6 oz / 1 cup quinoa, rinsed thoroughly in cold water and drained
- 1 lemon, juiced
- 1 tbsp extra-virgin olive oil
- 1 small cucumber, deseeded and finely diced
- 2 plum tomatoes, chopped
- 1 red pepper, deseeded and finely chopped
- a few mint leaves
- salt and pepper

Method

1. Place the quinoa in a large, heavy-based saucepan and gently cook over a low heat, stirring continuously until the grains separate.

2. Add 550 ml / 18 fl. oz / 2 ⅓ cups of cold water and a little salt, stir well, and bring to the boil.

3. Reduce to a simmer and cook for 15 minutes or until the liquid has been absorbed. Transfer to a mixing bowl and leave to cool.

4. Whisk together the lemon juice, seasoning and olive oil in a mixing bowl and dress the quinoa with it.

5. Add the cucumber, tomato and red pepper and fold gently but thoroughly into the quinoa.

6. Spoon into serving glasses and garnish with mint leaves before serving.

Top Tip

Try adding 50 g / 2 oz / ¼ cup chopped feta to the quinoa before serving.

Main Meals

Healthy eating can include more substantial meals than just salads and soups. These recipes are packed with fresh ingredients and healthy fats for all-round goodness. The rich Broccoli and Bacon Clafoutis is a creamy, meaty hotpot which will satisfy any naughty cravings you have.

For a juicy vegetable dish try the Bulghur-stuffed Peppers, served as a side or a main meal to add a splash of colour to your plate.

Top Tip

You can infuse the stock with a few saffron threads to change the colour of the risotto.

Artichoke and Tomato Risotto

Serves: **4** | Preparation time: **15 minutes**
Cooking time: **45–50 minutes** | Calorie content: **278–283 cal/portion**

Ingredients

- 2 tbsp sun-dried tomatoes
- 2 tbsp sunflower oil
- 2 shallots, finely chopped
- 2 cloves of garlic, minced
- 200 g / 7 oz / 2 cups Arborio rice
- 110 ml / 4 fl. oz / ½ cup dry white wine
- 1 l / 1 pint 16–18 fl. oz / 4–5 cups low sodium vegetable stock, kept hot on the stove
- 400 g / 14 oz / 2 cups canned artichoke hearts, drained and roughly chopped
- 1 small bunch of basil, leaves picked
- salt and pepper

Method

1. Soak the sun-dried tomatoes in boiling water for 10 minutes then drain, chop and set to one side.

2. Heat the oil in a saucepan set over a medium heat. Sauté the shallots gently for 4–5 minutes, then add the garlic and continue to cook for a further 2 minutes, stirring frequently.

3. Add the rice and coat in the oil. Cook for 3–4 minutes or until the grains start to turn translucent.

4. Add the white wine and increase the heat to allow it to evaporate almost entirely.

5. Add one ladle of stock at a time to the rice, stirring frequently, until each ladle has been absorbed into it.

6. Continue until all the stock has been absorbed and the rice is soft yet still defined. Usually 30–35 minutes.

7. Stir through the artichoke and sun-dried tomato to warm through. Adjust the seasoning to taste before serving with basil leaves on top.

Tofu Omelette

Serves: **4** | Preparation time: **5 minutes**
Cooking time: **12–15 minutes** | Calorie content: **133 cal/portion**

Ingredients

- non-fat cooking spray
- 6 medium eggs
- 55 ml / 2 fl. oz / ¼ cup skimmed (0%) milk
- 1 green pepper, deseeded and finely diced
- 150 g / 5 oz / 1 cup regular tofu (firm), diced
- a sprig of coriander (cilantro) leaves
- salt and pepper

Method

1. Preheat the oven to 180°C (160°C fan) / 350F / gas 4.

2. Coat a ovenproof sauté or omelette pan with cooking spray and place over a medium heat until hot.

3. Beat together the eggs and milk with a little seasoning in a jug and set to one side.

4. Sauté the green pepper for 2 minutes, stirring frequently, then pour in the egg.

5. Let it set for 1 minute before dotting the surface with tofu and transferring to the oven to finish cooking for 8–10 minutes until golden and puffed.

6. Remove from the oven and garnish with coriander before serving.

Top Tip

As an alternative to tofu, you can use cubes of reduced-fat Halloumi.

Top Tip

This salad can
be chilled and eaten
cold as well.

Cherry Tomato and Mint Pasta

Serves: **4** | Preparation time: **10 minutes**
Cooking time: **20 minutes** | Calorie content: **236 cal/portion**

Ingredients

- 225 g / 8 oz / 1 ½ cups cherry tomatoes on the vine
- 4 rashes of turkey bacon, halved
- 200 g / 7 oz / 3 cups pasta wheels
- 100 g / 3 ½ oz / 1 cup frozen petit pois, thawed
- 1 small bunch of mint, leaves picked
- salt and freshly ground black pepper

Method

1. Preheat the oven to 180°C (160°C fan) / 350F / gas 4 and line a baking tray with greaseproof paper.

2. Sit the cherry tomatoes on the tray and season before roasting. After 10 minutes, add the turkey bacon to the tray and return to the oven for 10 minutes.

3. Meanwhile, cook the pasta in a saucepan of salted, boiling water for 10 minutes until 'al dente' then drain well.

4. Toss the warm pasta with the petit pois to warm through then arrange in a serving bowl with the tomatoes and bacon.

5. Garnish with mint leaves and black pepper before serving.

Grilled Mediterranean Vegetables

Serves: **4** | Preparation time: **10 minutes**
Cooking time: **20 minutes** | Calorie content: **59 cal/portion**

Ingredients

- 2 large courgettes (zucchinis)
- 2 small aubergines (eggplants)
- 2 red peppers, deseeded and chopped
- 1 tbsp sunflower oil
- 1 tsp herbes de Provence
- salt and pepper

Method

1. Preheat the oven to 200°C (180°C fan) / 400F / gas 6.

2. Heat a griddle pan over a high heat and scorch the skins of the courgettes and aubergines, in batches, until coloured all over.

3. Cut the vegetables into slices and toss with the red pepper, oil, herbs de Provence and seasoning in a mixing bowl, then transfer to a roasting tin.

4. Roast for 20 minutes then remove and leave to cool a little before serving.

Top Tip

Mix a little pesto into fat-free crème fraiche and drizzle over before serving.

Top Tip

You can use green or yellow curry paste interchangeably in this recipe.

Chicken and Bean Curry

Serves: **4** | Preparation time: **10 minutes**
Cooking time: **35 minutes** | Calorie content: **175 cal/portion**

Ingredients

- non-fat cooking spray
- 2 cloves of garlic, chopped
- 2 tbsp Thai red curry paste
- 4 small vine tomatoes, cored and diced
- 3 large skinless chicken breasts, diced
- 500 ml / 18 fl. oz / 2 cups low sodium chicken stock
- 200 g / 7 oz / 2 cups French beans, trimmed
- 2 tsp sesame seeds
- salt and pepper

Method

1. Coat a medium casserole dish or saucepan with cooking spray and place over a medium heat.

2. Gently fry the garlic for 1 minute before adding the curry paste. Stir and cook for 1 minute then add the tomatoes and chicken.

3. Cook for 3–4 minutes, stirring occasionally, then cover with stock and stir well.

4. Bring the liquid to a simmer, reduce the heat to low and cook uncovered for 15 minutes.

5. Add the beans and continue to cook, covered with a lid, over a low heat for 8–10 minutes until they are tender.

6. Adjust the seasoning to taste before ladling into serving bowls and garnishing with sesame seeds.

Diet Beef Bourguignon

Serves: **4** | Preparation time: **15–20 minutes**
Cooking time: **1 ½–2 hours** | Calorie content: **275 cal/portion**

Ingredients

- non-fat cooking spray
- 1 tbsp sunflower oil
- 675 g / 1 lb 10 oz / 4 ½ cups lean beef stewing steak, diced
- 2 medium onions, finely chopped
- 2 cloves of garlic, minced
- 2 medium carrots, peeled and sliced
- 125 ml / 4 ½ fl. oz / ½ cup red wine
- 500 ml / 18 fl. oz / 2 cups low sodium beef stock
- 2 bouquet garni
- salt and freshly ground pepper

Method

1. Preheat the oven to 150°C (130°C fan) / 300F / gas 2.

2. Coat a large casserole dish with cooking spray and place over a moderate heat until hot.

3. Add the oil and seal the beef in batches until coloured all over.

4. Reduce the heat and add the onion, garlic and carrots. Sauté for 5–6 minutes, stirring frequently.

5. Add the wine, scraping the base well, before covering with stock. Add 1 bouquet garni and bring the liquid to a simmer then cover with a lid and transfer to the oven for 1½–2 hours until the beef is tender.

6. Remove the dish from the oven and adjust the seasoning to taste before spooning into bowls.

7. Garnish with another bouquet garni before serving.

Top Tip

Try adding some peeled pearl onions to the dish before cooking in the oven.

Top Tip

Try adding a small handful of raisins and a few flaked almonds to the bulghur before stuffing.

Bulghur-stuffed Peppers

Serves: **4** | Preparation time: **15–20 minutes**
Cooking time: **20–25 minutes** | Calories content: **146 cal/portion**

Ingredients

- 1 orange pepper
- 1 red pepper
- 1 green pepper
- 1 yellow pepper
- 150 g / 5 oz / ⅔ cup bulghur wheat, rinsed
- 250 ml / 9 fl. oz / 1 cup low sodium vegetable stock
- 1 small onion, finely chopped
- 1 small bunch of flat-leaf parsley, finely chopped
- salt and pepper

Method

1. Preheat the oven to 180°C (160°C fan) / 350F / gas 4.

2. Remove the tops of the peppers using a sharp knife and hollow out the main cavities, discarding the ribs and seeds. Reserve the tops.

3. Combine the bulghur and stock in a saucepan and cook over a low heat, stirring occasionally, until the bulghur has absorbed the liquid.

4. Add the onion and parsley and adjust the seasoning to taste.

5. Spoon the bulghur into the peppers and arrange standing up in a small roasting tray. Replace the lids and bake for 20–25 minutes until soft.

6. Remove and leave to stand for 5 minutes before serving.

Broccoli and Bacon Clafoutis

Serves: **4** | Preparation time: **15 minutes**
Cooking time: **25–30 minutes** | Calorie content: **253 cal/portion**

Ingredients

- non-fat cooking spray
- 50 g / 2 oz / ⅓ cup pancetta, diced
- 150 g / 5 oz / 1 cup plain (all purpose) flour, sifted
- 250 ml / 9 fl. oz / 1 cup skimmed (0%) milk
- 3 small eggs, beaten
- 350 g / 12 oz / 4 cups fresh broccoli florets
- 50 g / 2 oz / 1 cup baby spinach, washed and dried
- 4 tarragon sprigs, to serve
- salt and pepper

Method

1. Preheat the oven to 160°C (140°C fan) / 325F / gas 3 and coat the insides of 4 individual ramekins with cooking spray.

2. Heat a frying pan over a medium heat until hot and sauté the pancetta until golden. Drain on kitchen paper.

3. Place the flour and a little seasoning in a mixing bowl and whisk in the milk and eggs gradually until you have a batter.

4. Fill the ramekins with broccoli carefully pour in the batter. Dot with pancetta.

5. Bake for 25–30 minutes until the clafoutis are set.

6. Remove from the oven and leave to cool for a few minutes before serving with spinach on the side and a tarragon sprig on top.

Top Tip

Swap the pancetta for diced cherry tomatoes for a vegetarian version of this dish.

Top Tip

This salad can work equally well with turkey breast or escalopes.

Chicken and Apple Salad

Serves: **4** | Preparation time: **10–15 minutes**
Cooking time: **20–25 minutes** | Calorie content: **197 cal/portion**

Ingredients

- 1 tbsp sunflower oil
- 2 large chicken breasts
- 2 small slices of wholemeal bread
- 100 g / 3 ½ oz / 2 cups lamb's lettuce
- 2 small Granny Smith apples, cored and finely sliced
- 1 large carrot, peeled and finely grated
- 1 tbsp sultanas
- 30 g / 1 oz / ¼ cup reduced fat Cheddar, cut into cubes
- salt and pepper

Method

1. Preheat the oven to 180°C (160°C fan) / 350F / gas 4 and line a baking tray with greaseproof paper.

2. Sit the chicken breasts on it and coat with the oil. Season generously.

3. Roast for 20–25 minutes until cooked through then remove from the oven and leave to rest for 5–10 minutes.

4. Meanwhile, toast the slices of bread until golden on both sides then cut into croutons.

5. Remove the skin from the chicken and cut into slices.

6. Arrange in serving dishes with the lamb's lettuce, apple, carrot, sultanas and Cheddar. Garnish with croutons before serving.

Warm Pasta Salad

Serves: **4** | Preparation time: **5–10 minutes**
Cooking time: **10–15 minutes** | Calorie content: **178 cal/portion**

Ingredients

- 150 g / 5 oz / 2 cups orecchiette pasta
- 1 tbsp sunflower oil
- 1 small courgette (zucchini), deseeded and finely diced
- 1 red pepper, deseeded and finely diced
- 1 yellow pepper, deseeded and finely diced
- 1 tbsp Parmesan, grated
- a small handful of rocket (arugula)
- salt and freshly ground black pepper

Method

1. Cook the pasta in a large saucepan of salted, boiling water for 8–11 minutes until 'al dente'. Drain well, reserving half a mug of cooking water.

2. Heat the oil in a large saucepan set over a medium heat until hot and gently fry the courgette and peppers until slightly softened.

3. Add the pasta to the saucepan as well as the cooking water and stir well, cooking over a low heat for a further minute.

4. Adjust the seasoning to taste before spooning into serving bowls and topping with Parmesan, rocket and black pepper.

5. Serve immediately for best results.

Top Tip

Swap the vegetables
for diced red onion
and chopped sun-dried
tomatoes for a
textural contrast.

Top Tip

Try adding pitted green and black olives to the parcels before baking.

Haddock en Papillote

Serves: **4** | Preparation time: **10–15 minutes**
Cooking time: **15 minutes** | Calorie content: **204 cal/portion**

Ingredients

- 150 g / 5 oz / 1 ½ cups mange tout
- 2 medium carrots, peeled and sliced
- 4 x 150 g / 5 oz / ¾ cup haddock fillets, skinless
- 1 tbsp olive oil
- 150 g / 5 oz / 1 cup new potatoes, halved
- 1 lemon, sliced
- a few sprigs of dill, chopped
- ½ tsp red peppercorns, crushed
- salt and pepper

Method

1. Preheat the oven to 180°C (160°C fan) / 350F / gas 4.
2. Cut out squares of greaseproof paper approximately 30 cm x 30 cm (12 in x 12 in) in size and place the mange tout and carrot in the middle.
3. Sit the haddock on top and drizzle with a little oil. Season generously then bring the sides of the paper up and over the fish, folding them together to make sealed parcels.
4. Place on a baking tray and bake for 10–15 minutes until cooked through.
5. Meanwhile, cook the potatoes in a saucepan of salted, boiling water for 10–15 minutes until tender then drain.
6. Arrange the potatoes, mange tout, carrot and lemon slices in serving bowls and sit the fish on top.
7. Garnish with dill and a pinch of red peppercorns before serving.

Desserts

Indulgent sweets and treats don't have to be fattening and laden with calories. Try these mouth-watering, guilt-free desserts and you won't have to worry about piling on the pounds.

The Strawberry Salad with Lemon Sorbet is ideal for any blissful summer evening in the garden. Or try the Low-carb Muffins which are great for sharing at parties and with the family.

Low-fat Cocoa Millefeuilles

Serves: **4** | Preparation time: **15–20 minutes**
Cooking time: **10–12 minutes** | Calorie content: **193 cal/portion**

Ingredients

- 250 ml / 9 fl. oz / 1 cup semi-skimmed (2%) milk
- 250 ml / 9 fl. oz/ 1 cup skimmed (0%) milk
- 1 tsp vanilla extract
- 45 g / 1 ½ oz / ⅓ cup instant custard powder
- 40 g / 1 ½ oz / ¼ cup stevia or granulated sweetener
- 100 g / 3 ½ oz / ½ cup ready-made lighter puff pastry
- a little plain (all purpose) flour, for dusting
- 2 tbsp cocoa powder

Method

1. Combine the milks and vanilla extract in a medium saucepan set over moderate heat, and combine the custard powder and sweetener in a measuring jug. Add 2–3 tbsp of the milk from the saucepan and stir until smooth.

2. Once the milk nears boiling, slowly pour it over the paste, whisking continuously.

3. Stir the custard for 1 minute before leaving to cool and thicken.

4. Preheat the oven to 190°C (170°C fan) / 375F / gas 5 and line a baking tray with greaseproof paper.

5. Roll out the pastry on a floured surface to ½ cm thickness; cut into twelve 8 cm x 2 cm (3 ½ in x 1 in) rectangles and arrange on the tray. Prick with a fork before baking for 10–12 minutes until golden.

6. Remove from the oven and trim the edges, then top 8 with custard. Stack them in pairs and place the remaining 4 pastry slices on top to make the millefeuilles.

7. Dust with cocoa before chilling and serving.

Top Tip

Replace the cocoa powder on top with a drizzle of raspberry sauce.

Top Tip

Sprinkle the tops of the muffins with oat bran just before baking for a crunchy top.

Low-carb Muffins

Serves: **12** | Preparation time: **10 minutes**
Cooking time: **20–25 minutes** | Calorie content: **81 cal/portion**

Ingredients

- 125 g / 4 ½ oz / ¾ cup cornflour (cornstarch)
- 110 g / 4 oz / ⅔ cup oat bran, ground
- 75 g / 3 oz / ½ cup stevia or granulated sweetener
- 100 g / 3 ½ oz / ½ cup fat-free Greek yoghurt
- 1 tsp vanilla extract
- ½ tsp baking powder
- 2 medium eggs
- 2 medium egg whites
- two pinches of salt

Method

1. Preheat the oven to 180°C (160°C fan) / 350F / gas 4 and line a 12-hole muffin tray with cases.

2. Place all the ingredients, apart from the egg whites and one pinch of salt, in a food processor and pulse until roughly combined.

3. Spoon the mixture into a bowl and beat the egg whites in a separate, clean bowl with a pinch of salt, until stiff peaks form.

4. Fold the whites into the other bowl of ingredients and spoon the batter into the cases.

5. Bake for 20–25 minutes until golden and risen; test with a wooden toothpick, if it comes out clean, the muffins are done.

6. Remove the tray to a wire rack to cool before serving the muffins.

Rosemary-roasted Apricots

Serves: **4** | Preparation time: **5–10 minutes**
Cooking time: **30–40 minutes** | Calorie content: **132 cal/portion**

Ingredients

- 800 g / 1 lb 12 oz / 4 cups canned apricot halves in syrup, drained with juice reserved
- 55 ml / 2 fl. oz / ¼ cup lemon juice
- ½ tsp dried rosemary
- 4 sprigs of rosemary

Method

1. Preheat the oven to 180°C (160°C fan) / 350F / gas 4.

2. Neatly arrange the apricot halves in a roasting tin. Stir together the reserved juice with the lemon juice and dried rosemary.

3. Pour the liquid over the apricots, then tuck the rosemary sprigs in and around the them.

4. Roast for 30–40 minutes until the apricots are lightly coloured on top.

5. Remove from the oven and leave to cool a little before serving in bowls with some of the cooking liquor spooned over them.

Top Tip

Canned peaches or nectarines work equally well in this recipe.

Top Tip

Serve the fruits with a dollop of Greek yoghurt or frozen yoghurt instead of meringue.

Summer Fruits with Meringue

Serves: **4** | Preparation time: **15 minutes**
Cooking time: **15–20 minutes** | Calorie content: **93 cal/portion**

Ingredients

- 1 large egg white
- a pinch of salt
- 55 g / 2 oz / ¼ cup caster (superfine) sugar
- 150 g / 5 oz / 1 cup strawberries, hulled and halved
- 75 g / 3 oz / ¾ cup redcurrants
- 110 g / 4 oz / ¾ cup blueberries
- 75 ml / 3 fl. oz / ⅓ cup cold water
- 1 tbsp stevia or granulated sweetener

Method

1. Preheat the oven to 180°C (160°C fan) / 350F / gas 4 and line a baking tray with greaseproof paper.
2. Beat the egg white with a pinch of salt in a clean, grease-free bowl until stiff peaks form.
3. Beat in the sugar, one tablespoon at a time, until you have a thick, glossy meringue.
4. Spoon the meringue onto the baking tray in four mounds and bake for 15–20 minutes until coloured on top and set.
5. Meanwhile, combine the fruits with the water and stevia in a small saucepan. Stir once.
6. Cover with a lid and cook over a very low heat for 10 minutes.
7. Remove the meringue from the oven and leave to cool a little.
8. Spoon the fruit and any juices from the saucepan into serving bowls before topping with a mound of meringue and serving.

Crunchy Raspberry-topped Scones

Serves: **8** | Preparation time: **15–20 minutes**
Cooking time: **14–16 minutes** | Calorie content: **166 cal/portion**

Ingredients

- 225 g / 8 oz / 1 ½ cups plain (all purpose) flour, sifted
- ½ tsp baking powder
- ½ tsp bicarbonate of (baking) soda
- 1 tbsp stevia or granulated sweetener
- 55 g / 2 oz / ¼ cup reduced fat margarine
- 150 ml / 5 fl. oz / ⅔ cup semi-skimmed (2%) milk
- 1 tbsp mint leaves, finely chopped
- 2 tbsp finely grated lime zest
- 350 g / 12 oz / 3 cups raspberries
- 125 g / 4 ½ oz / ½ cup fat-free Greek yoghurt

Method

1. Preheat the oven to 200°C (180°C fan) / 400F / gas 6 and line a large baking tray with greaseproof paper.

2. Stir together the flour, baking powder, bicarbonate of soda and stevia in a mixing bowl.

3. Rub in the margarine and add the milk, mint and lime zest, mixing until a soft dough forms. Knead briefly then pat into a 1 cm (½ in) thick round and cut out 8 rounds, approximately 5 cm (2 in) in diameter.

4. Arrange on the baking tray and bake for 14–16 minutes until slightly risen and coloured at the edges.

5. Remove from the oven to a wire rack to cool.

6. Puree a large handful of raspberries with the Greek yoghurt in a food processor, then press through a fine sieve and spooning on top of the scones.

7. Top with the remaining raspberries before serving.

Top Tip

Replace the mint and lime zest with a large handful of sultanas for a chewier texture.

Top Tip

Scatter a few raisins
on top of the apple
before baking.

Thin
Apple Tart

Serves: **4** | Preparation time: **15 minutes**
Cooking time: **20–25 minutes** | Calorie content: **195 cal/portion**

Ingredients

- 100 g / 3 ½ oz / ½ cup ready-made lighter shortcrust pastry
- a little plain (all purpose) flour, for dusting
- 2 medium Granny Smith apples, peeled, cored and thinly sliced
- 2 tbsp caster (superfine) sugar
- 1 tsp ground cinnamon
- 110 g / 4 oz / ⅔ cup plain frozen yoghurt, to serve

Method

1. Preheat the oven to 180°C (160°C fan) / 350F / gas 4 and line a baking tray with greaseproof paper.

2. Roll out the pastry on a lightly floured surface to ½ cm thickness. Cut out 4 squares approximately 10 cm x 10 cm (4 in x 4 in).

3. Transfer to the baking tray and prick all over with a fork.

4. Top with slices of apple and a sprinkling of sugar before baking for 20–25 minutes until the pastry is cooked through and the apples are lightly coloured.

5. Remove from the oven and dust with cinnamon before serving with a scoop of frozen yoghurt on top.

Strawberry Salad with Lemon Sorbet

Serves: **8** | Preparation time: **2–3 hours**

Cooking time: **10 minutes** | Calorie content: **152 cal/portion**

Ingredients

- 175 ml / 6 fl. oz / ¾ cup cold water
- 110 g / 4 oz / ½ cup caster (superfine) sugar
- 175 ml / 6 fl. oz / ¾ cup lemon juice
- 1 tbsp grated lemon zest
- 400 g / 14 oz / 3 cups strawberries, hulled and halved
- 50 ml / 2 fl. oz / ¼ cup balsamic vinegar
- a pinch of ground black pepper

Method

1. Combine the water and the sugar in a saucepan set over a moderate heat, stirring occasionally, until the sugar has dissolved.

2. Cook the syrup for 1 minute, then remove from the heat and leave to cool.

3. Stir in the lemon juice and zest once cool and pour into a 30 cm x 20 cm (12 in x 8 in) metal baking dish. Freeze for 2–3 hours, stirring with a fork every 30 minutes.

4. Meanwhile, combine the strawberries with the vinegar and pepper in a mixing bowl.

5. Stir well, cover and chill for at least 1 hour.

6. Spoon the marinated salad into serving glasses and top with sorbet before serving.

Top Tip

You can substitute the lemon juice for lime or orange for a different citrus flavour.

Top Tip

Replace the redcurrants with blackcurrants for a different taste.

Red Fruit Millefeuilles

Serves: **4** | Preparation time: **15 minutes**
Cooking time: **8–10 minutes** | Calorie content: **217 cal/portion**

Ingredients

- 50 g / 2 oz / ¼ cup unsalted butter, softened
- 40 g / 1 ½ oz / ¼ cup stevia
- a few drops of vanilla extract
- 2 small egg whites
- 50 g / 2 oz / ⅓ cup plain (all purpose) flour, sifted
- 200 g / 8 oz / 1 cup quark
- 150 g / 5 oz / 1 cup strawberries, sliced
- 100 g / 3 ½ oz / ⅔ cup raspberries
- 50 g / 2 oz / ½ cup redcurrants
- 1 tbsp icing (confectioners') sugar

Method

1. Preheat the oven to 180°C (160°C fan) / 350F / gas 4 and line a large baking tray with greaseproof paper.

2. Beat together the butter, stevia and vanilla extract in a bowl until smooth.

3. Beat in the egg whites until incorporated and follow with the flour, stirring until smooth.

4. Spread the mixture in 12 rounds onto the greaseproof paper, then bake for 8–10 minutes until golden. Remove and leaving to cool.

5. Beat the quark in a small bowl until smooth and creamy then spread onto 8 of the tuiles and top with a mixture of the red fruits.

6. Stack the topped tuiles in pairs then place the remaining plain tuiles on top.

7. Dust with icing sugar before serving.

Individual Cheesecakes

Serves: **4** | Preparation time: **10–15 minutes**
Cooking time: **25–35 minutes** | Calorie content: **239 cal/portion**

Ingredients

- 75 g / 3 oz / ½ cup reduced fat digestive (graham cracker) biscuits, crushed

- 2 tbsp reduced fat margarine, melted

- a pinch of salt

- 1 tbsp dark chocolate, finely chopped

- 225 g / 8 oz / 1 cup fat-free cream cheese, softened

- 75 g / 3 oz / ½ cup stevia or granulated sweetener

- 110 g / 4 oz / ½ cup fat-free sour cream

- 2 tsp vanilla extract

- 2 medium eggs

Method

1. Preheat the oven to 160°C (140°C fan) / 325F / gas 3 and arrange 4 individual heatproof ramekins in a roasting tin.

2. Combine the biscuits, melted margarine and salt in a small bowl before pressing three quarters of the mixture into the base of the ramekins.

3. Top with a little chocolate then chill as you prepare the filling.

4. Beat together the cream cheese, stevia and sour cream until smooth, add the vanilla extract and then beat in the eggs one at a time.

5. Divide the mixture between the ramekins before half-filling the roasting tin with hot water.

6. Bake for 25–35 minutes until the filling is just set. Remove, cover and chill overnight.

7. Serve with a little more of the biscuit mixture and chocolate sprinkled on top.

Top Tip

Substitute the dark chocolate for 1 tbsp chopped crystallised ginger for an exotic touch.

Top Tip

Add ½ tsp peppermint
extract to the soup
for a fresh hit.

Strawberry Granita Soup

Serves: **4** | Preparation time: **2–3 hours**
Cooking time: **10 minutes** | Calorie content: **108 cal/portion**

Ingredients

- 1 l / 1 pint 16 fl. oz / 4 cups cold water
- 75 g / 3 oz / ⅓ cup caster (superfine) sugar
- 450 g / 1 lb / 3 cups strawberries, hulled and chopped
- 2 tbsp lemon juice
- a few sprigs of sage leaves

Method

1. Combine the water and sugar in a saucepan set over a moderate heat.

2. Heat the mixture, stirring frequently, until the sugar has dissolved. Add strawberries and lemon juice and stir well before cooking for a further 2 minutes then remove from the heat.

3. Let the mixture cool then strain half of the liquid into a metal baking dish or tin. Freeze for 2–3 hours, stirring with a fork every 30 minutes, until set.

4. Cover and chill the remaining strawberry soup as the granita freezes.

5. Once the granita is ready, divide the strawberry soup between four serving glasses and top with granita.

6. Garnish with sage leaves before serving.

Summer Fruit and Thyme Soup

Serves: **4** | Preparation time: **1 hour 10 minutes**
Cooking time: **5–10 minutes** | Calorie content: **50 cal/portion**

Ingredients

- 750 ml / 1 pint 6 fl. oz / 3 cups cold water
- 75 g / 3 oz / ½ cup stevia or granulated sweetener
- 2 tbsp lemon juice
- 150 g / 5 oz / 1 cup strawberries, hulled and halved
- 150 g / 5 oz / 1 ⅓ cups raspberries
- 110 g / 4 oz / 1 cup blackberries
- a few sprigs of lemon thyme

Method

1. Combine the water and sweetener in a saucepan set over a moderate heat.

2. Heat until the sweetener dissolves, stirring frequently, then add the lemon juice, half of the strawberries, blackberries, raspberries and the lemon thyme.

3. Stir briefly then remove from the heat. Let the soup cool before covering and chilling for 1 hour.

4. Divide the soup between 4 serving bowls and arrange the remaining fruit in them before serving.

Top Tip

Try different herbs such as tarragon instead of lemon thyme.

Snacks and Drinks

These bite-size snacks are packed with all kinds of goodness. If you need a quick fix then the Carrot, Ginger and Orange Lassi can be whipped up in a matter of minutes.

There are a range of sweet and savoury bites which will make delicious aperitifs for a special dinner. If you fancy a decadent yummy treat, then the Shrimp Canapés are a real crowd-pleaser.

Top Tip

Add a thinly sliced red onion to the tomatoes before grilling for colour and texture.

Tomato and Turkey Bacon Bruschetta

Serves: **4** | Preparation time: **10 minutes**
Cooking time: **5–6 minutes** | Calorie content: **200 cal/portion**

Ingredients

- 4 small vine tomatoes, cored
- 4 slices of white sourdough bread, 2–3 cm (1–1 ½ in) thick
- 1 tbsp extra-virgin olive oil
- 75 g / 3 oz / ½ cup turkey bacon
- 50 g / 2 oz / 1 cup rocket (arugula) leaves
- salt and pepper

Method

1. Preheat the grill to hot and place a grilling tray underneath the get hot.

2. Cut the tomatoes in half and deseed them before chopping.

3. Lightly brush the slices of sourdough with olive oil, then grilling them on the preheated tray for 1 minute on both sides.

4. Remove and top with the tomatoes and bacon before returning to the grill for 3–4 minutes until the bacon is cooked and sizzling.

5. Remove from the grill and season a little and cut in half.

6. Garnish with rocket leaves on top before serving.

Stuffed Vine Tomatoes

Serves: **4** | Preparation time: **10 minutes**
Calorie content: **95 cal/portion**

Ingredients

- 4 large vine tomatoes
- 225 g / 8 oz / 1 cup fat-free cream cheese
- 1 small courgette (zucchini), finely chopped
- ½ tsp red chilli (chili) flakes
- salt and pepper

Method

1. Cut the tomatoes horizontally in half and scoop out most of the seeds from the bottom halves.

2. Beat the cream cheese until smooth in a mixing bowl and add half of the courgette and the chilli flakes.

3. Stir again and season to taste, then use it to fill the bottom halves of the tomatoes.

4. Stud the filling with the remaining courgette and chilli flakes and replace the top halves.

5. Serve cold.

Top Tip

Try adding half a chopped yellow pepper to the cream cheese.

Top Tip

The prosciutto can
be replaced with
sun-dried tomato for
a vegetarian version.

Three-topping Bruschettas

Serves: **6** | Preparation time: **10 minutes**
Cooking time: **4–5 minutes** | Calorie content: **213 cal/portion**

Ingredients

- 6 slices of white sourdough bread, 2–3 (1–1 ½ in) cm thick
- 150 g / 5 oz / 1 cup reduced-fat mozzarella, drained
- 50 g / 2 oz / 1 cup baby spinach leaves, washed and dried
- 75 g / 3 oz / ¾ cup prosciutto slices
- freshly ground black pepper

Method

1. Preheat the grill to hot and place a grilling tray under it.

2. Once hot, arrange the pieces of sourdough on it and grill them for 1 minute on both sides. Remove and leave to cool on a wire rack.

3. Pat the mozzarella dry and divide into six pieces reserving any offcuts.

4. Assemble the bruschetta by placing a piece of mozzarella in the centre of the toasted sourdough.

5. Season with black pepper and top with spinach leaves, then fold the prosciutto and placing it on top.

6. Arrange any offcuts of mozzarella on top and grill for 2–3 minutes until the cheese starts to melt and the prosciutto starts to colour.

7. Remove from the grill and serve immediately.

Chilli Tofu Appetizers

Serves: **4** | Preparation time: **5 minutes**
Cooking time: **5 minutes** | Calorie content: **51 cal/portion**

Ingredients

- 2 tbsp sunflower oil
- 225 g / 8 oz / 2 cups pressed tofu, cubed
- 1 tsp chilli (chili) powder
- 1 tsp ground star anise
- 30 g / 1 oz / ½ cup beansprouts
- salt and pepper

Method

1. Coat the tofu in the oil and sprinkle over half the chilli powder, the ground star anise and seasoning. Toss well.

2. Heat a large frying pan over a moderate heat until hot and pan-fry the tofu until golden-brown in colour all over, around 3–4 minutes.

3. Drain on kitchen paper then arrange on serving plates and garnishing with a dusting of the remaining chilli powder and some beansprouts.

Top Tip

Crush 1 tsp pink peppercorns and use instead of the chilli powder before pan-frying the tofu.

Top Tip

You can replace the steamed shrimp with flaked smoked mackerel fillets.

Guacamole and Shrimp Canapés

Serves: **4** | Preparation time: **10 minutes**
Cooking time: **7–10 minutes** | Calorie content: **104 cal/portion**

Ingredients

- 1 large ripe avocado, pitted, peeled and chopped
- 1 lime, juiced
- ½ clove of garlic, minced
- 1 tsp hot sauce
- 200 g / 7 oz / 1 ⅓ cups whole shrimp, peeled and deveined
- 6 rectangular saltine or cream crackers
- a pinch of cayenne pepper
- a few sprigs of coriander (cilantro)
- salt and pepper

Method

1. Prepare the guacamole by mashing together the avocado flesh with the lime juice, garlic and hot sauce.
2. Adjust the seasoning to taste, then cover and chill.
3. Place the shrimp in a steaming basket and cover with a lid and set atop a saucepan of simmering water.
4. Let the steam cook the shrimp until pink and tender, approximately 7–10 minutes.
5. Remove from the basket and pat dry before seasoning.
6. Spread the guacamole onto the crackers and top with a pinch of cayenne pepper and a couple of shrimp.
7. Garnish with coriander before serving.

Bran Muffins

Makes: **12** | Preparation time: **10–15 minutes**
Cooking time: **20–25 minutes** | Calorie content: **107 cal/portion**

Ingredients

- 200 g / 7 oz / 1 ⅓ cups plain (all purpose) flour
- 75 g / 3 oz / ½ cup wheat bran
- 110 g / 4 oz / ⅔ cup stevia or granulated sweetener
- 1 tbsp pumpkin seeds
- 2 tsp baking powder
- ½ tsp salt
- 225 ml / 8 fl. oz / 1 cup skimmed (0%) milk
- 110 ml / 4 fl. oz / ½ cup sunflower oil
- 1 small egg

Method

1. Preheat the oven to 180°C (160°C fan) / 350F / gas 4 and line a 12-hole muffin tin with large cases.

2. Combine the flour, wheat bran, stevia, pumpkin seeds, baking powder and salt in a large mixing bowl, then stir well.

3. Whisk together the milk, oil and egg in a jug and add to the dry ingredients, mixing until the batter comes together – it should still be lumpy and not over-mixed.

4. Spoon the batter into the cases and tap the tin a few times to help the batter settle.

5. Bake for 20–25 minutes until ready. A cake tester inserted in the centre should come out clean.

6. Remove the muffins to a wire rack before serving or storing in an airtight container.

Top Tip

Try substituting
the pumpkin seeds
for a handful of
dried cranberries.

Top Tip

Try adding a handful of goji berries to the cookie dough for some colour.

Dukan Tofu Cookies

Makes: **12** | Preparation time: **15 minutes**
Cooking time: **14–16 minutes** | Calorie content: **53 cal/portion**

Ingredients

- 110 g / 4 oz / ⅔ cup regular tofu (firm)
- 200 g / 7 oz / 2 cups oat bran
- 75 g / 3 oz / ½ cup stevia or granulated sweetener
- a few mint leaves, finely chopped
- ½ tsp ground cinnamon
- ½ tsp baking powder
- ½ tsp bicarbonate of (baking) soda
- a pinch of salt
- 110 g / 4 oz / ½ cup fat-free Greek yoghurt
- 1 tsp vanilla extract

Method

1. Preheat the oven to 180°C (160°C fan) / 350F / gas 4 and line a large baking tray with greaseproof paper.

2. Pat the tofu dry and pulse in a food processor until finely chopped.

3. Tip into a bowl along with the oat bran, stevia, mint, cinnamon, baking powder, bicarbonate of soda and salt.

4. Stir well, then incorporate the Greek yoghurt and vanilla extract until you have a rough cookie dough. Add a little water if it seems too stiff.

5. Shape the mixture into rounds and arrange, spaced apart, on the baking tray. Bake for 14–16 minutes until golden-brown and set.

6. Remove from the oven and leave to cool before serving.

Cucumber Ices with Limeade

Serves: **6** | Preparation time: **3–4 hours**
Calorie content: **28 cal/portion**

Ingredients

- 2 medium cucumbers, thinly sliced
- 1 small bunch of mint leaves, picked
- 225 ml / 8 fl. oz / 1 cup freshly squeezed lime juice
- 75 g / 3 oz / ½ cup stevia or granulated sweetener
- 1 l / 1 pint 16 fl. oz / 4 cups sparkling (soda) water, chilled
- 1 lime, halved and cut into slices

Method

1. Blitz together most of the cucumber, apart from 6 slices, with three-quarters of the mint leaves in a food processor.

2. Press the puree through a sieve, collecting the liquid in a bowl. Stir in half of the lime juice and half of the stevia.

3. Divide the liquid between 6 ice lolly moulds and freeze for one hour.

4. Remove after 1 hour and sit a slice of cucumber on top of each as well as skewering a lolly stick into them.

5. Return to the freezer for 2–3 hours until frozen.

6. Once frozen, run the moulds under hot water until the ices start to come free.

7. Mix together the remaining lime juice and stevia in a jug before slowly stirring in the sparkling water.

8. Pour into glasses and garnish with lime slices and the remaining mint leaves; serve alongside the ices.

Top Tip

Stir in 1 tsp dried chilli (chili) flakes to the cucumber mixture, before freezing, for a kick.

Top Tip

Try substituting the chilli flakes for a pinch of celery salt.

Spicy Tomato and Pepper Juice

Serves: **4** | Preparation time: **5–10 minutes**
Cooking time: **5–10 minutes** | Calorie content: **44 cal/portion**

Ingredients

- 450 g / 1 lb / 3 cups vine tomatoes, cored and chopped
- 2 red chillies (chilies), deseeded and chopped
- 225 g / 8 oz / 1 cup passata
- 250 ml / 9 fl. oz / 1 cup cold water
- 30 ml / 1 fl. oz / 2 tbsp lemon juice
- 1 tbsp hot sauce
- 1 tsp black peppercorns, lightly crushed
- ½ tsp red chilli (chili) flakes
- salt, to taste

Method

1. Place the chopped tomatoes and chopped chillies in a food processor and blitz for 25–30 seconds.

2. Strain the mixture through a fine sieve into a jug then stir in the water, passata, lemon juice and hot sauce.

3. Adjust the seasoning to taste, then cover and chill until cold.

4. Pour into glasses and garnish with black peppercorns and a pinch of chilli flakes before serving.

Assorted Fruit Smoothies

Serves: **6** | Preparation time: **5–10 minutes**

Calorie content: **192 cal/portion**

Ingredients

- 350 g / 12 oz / 2 ⅓ cups strawberries, hulled and halved

- 1 small banana, chopped

- 325 g / 11 oz / 1 ½ cups fat-free plain yoghurt

- 350 ml / 12 fl. oz / 1 ½ cups skimmed (0%) milk, chilled

- 200 g / 7 oz / 1 cup ice cubes

- 400 g / 14 oz / 2 cups canned mango slices, drained

- 400 g / 14 oz / 2 cups canned peach slices, drained

Method

1. For the strawberry smoothies, combine the strawberries and banana with one third of the yoghurt, milk and ice cubes in a smoothie maker or blender.

2. Blitz until smooth then pour into 2 disposable cups.

3. Blitz together the mango slices with half of the remaining yoghurt, milk and ice cubes until smooth. Pour into 2 disposable cups.

4. Blitz the remaining yoghurt, milk and ice cubes with the peach slices until smooth. Pour into disposable cups.

5. Serve immediately for best results.

Top Tip

You can add a tablespoon of rolled oats to each smoothie before blending for a thicker result.

Top Tip

Garnish the lassis
with a pinch of ground
coriander for an added
Indian twist.

Carrot, Ginger and Orange Lassi

Serves: **4** | Preparation time: **5–10 minutes**
Cooking time: **10–15 minutes** | Calories content: **179 cal/portion**

Ingredients

- 3 small carrots, peeled
- 5 cm (2 in) piece of ginger, peeled and chopped
- 250 g / 9 oz / 1 cup fat-free plain yoghurt
- 750 ml / 1 pint 6 fl. oz / 3 cups skimmed (0%) milk, chilled
- 150 ml / 5 fl. oz / ⅔ cup freshly squeezed orange juice
- a pinch of salt

Method

1. If you have a juicer, juice the carrots with the ginger, collecting the juice.

2. Combine with the yoghurt, milk, orange juice and a pinch of salt in a food processor or blender and pulse until combined.

3. If you don't have a juicer, place the carrots in a steamer, sitting over a saucepan of simmering water. Cook for 7–8 minutes until soft.

4. Chop the carrots and blitz with the ginger, yoghurt, milk, orange juice and a pinch of salt in a food processor until smooth.

5. Pass through a sieve and serve immediately for best results.

Index